CW01003369

Great Authors

a book of postcards

Library of Congress

Pomegranate Artbooks • San Francisco

Pomegranate Artbooks
Box 6099
Rohnert Park, CA 94927

ISBN 1-56640-649-8
Pomegranate Catalog No. A703

Pomegranate publishes books of postcards on a wide range of subjects.
Please write to the publisher for more information.

© 1993 Library of Congress

Designed by Allen Boyce Eddington
Printed in Korea

This second volume of *Great Authors: A Book of Postcards* draws its photographs and text from the vast resources of the Library of Congress. With the support of the U.S. Congress and private donors and collectors, the Library acquires research materials from around the globe and in more than 450 languages. It is the largest library in the world, holding over 100 million items including at least 20 million books. The Library also seeks to stimulate public interest in books, reading, literacy and libraries. Through the activities of the Center for the Book in the Library of Congress, through poetry and literature readings, lectures, children's literature readings and a wide variety of publications—such as this book of postcards—the Library seeks to remind the widest possible audience of the importance of writers and how the books they create can forever change the lives of those who read.

Great Authors

Nathaniel Hawthorne (American, 1804–1864). While crafting tales that established the American short story as an art form and creating such classic novels as *The Scarlet Letter* and *The House of Seven Gables,* Hawthorne also worked as a salt and coal measurer in Boston, as port surveyor in Salem and for four years as U.S. consul in Liverpool, England.

Pomegranate, Box 6099, Rohnert Park, CA 94927

Brady-Handy Collection, Prints and Photographs Division

Great Authors

Thomas Mann (German, 1875–1955). A writer of great
intellectual breadth, and of firm moral and political
sensibilities, Mann was deprived of his German
citizenship by the Nazis in 1936 after he openly
denounced them as "enemies of Christianity, of
Occidental morality, and of civilization itself." The
author of *Buddenbrooks* and *Death in Venice*, Mann is
generally regarded as one of the greatest writers of the
twentieth century.

Pomegranate, Box 6099, Rohnert Park, CA 94927

Photograph by Florence Homolka
Agnes Meyer Collection, Prints and Photographs Division
© Library of Congress

Great Authors

Booker T. (Taliaferro) Washington (American, 1859–1915) grew up and tenaciously pursued an education in the turbulent Reconstruction era. He worked in salt furnaces and coal mines to get the means to travel to the Hampton Institute, and he worked as a janitor there for his room and board. He became organizer and principal of Tuskegee Institute in 1881 and authored a number of books, including the admirable autobiography *Up from Slavery*. Washington was also one of the ablest public speakers of his time.

Pomegranate, Box 6099, Rohnert Park, CA 94927

Great Authors

Gertrude Stein (American, 1874–1946). A writer of
remarkably obscure prose, Gertrude Stein was a person
of powerful intellect and firm opinions ("Rose is a rose
is a rose is a rose"). She studied medicine for four years
at Johns Hopkins University, taking no degree. After
1903, she lived in France, where she came to wield great
influence in the worlds of art and words. She authored
The Autobiography of Alice B. Toklas and *The Making of
Americans*, among other books.

Pomegranate, Box 6099, Rohnert Park, CA 94927

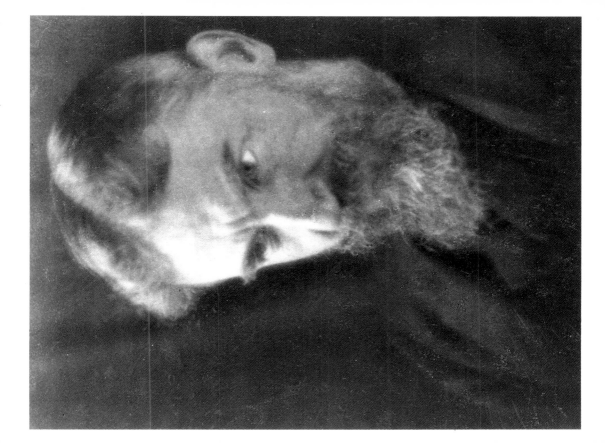

Great Authors

George Bernard Shaw (Irish, 1856–1950) created plays, novels, political prose, essays and criticism of such depth, wit and dramatic flair that a new adjective, *Shavian*, was coined to describe his particular combination of gifts. He was awarded the Nobel Prize in literature in 1925, his body of work by that time including some of his most brilliant plays, among them *Pygmalion*, *Arms and the Man* and *St. Joan.*

Pomegranate, Box 6099, Rohnert Park, CA 94927

Great Authors

William Butler Yeats (Irish, 1865–1939). Passionate in the creation of poetry, in experimentation with drama, in expression of his beliefs and detestation of pretense; foolish, perhaps, in his interest in the occult—Nobel laureate William Butler Yeats produced poems of increasing power and depth as his years progressed. He became a member of the Irish Senate, was cofounder of the Abbey Theatre, encouraged younger writers and was a critic, essayist and autobiographer.

Pomegranate, Box 6099, Rohnert Park, CA 94927

Great Authors

Isak Dinesen (The Baroness Blixen, Danish, 1885–1962). *Out of Africa* is perhaps Isak Dinesen's best-known work, the story of her seventeen years on a coffee plantation in what was then British East Africa. She is celebrated as a master storyteller whose work (*Seven Gothic Tales, Winter Tales, Last Tales*) is often touched by the supernatural.

Pomegranate, Box 6099, Rohnert Park, CA 94927

Great Authors

Anatole France (Jacques Anatole François Thibault, French, 1844–1924). Novelist, critic, 1921 Nobel laureate in literature, and a man of deep erudition and profound skepticism, Anatole France wrote mischievous short stories, provoking meditations and historical, philosophical and autobiographical novels crafted with grace and wit. "To know is nothing at all," he wrote in *The Crime of Sylvestre Bonnard*; "to imagine is everything."

Pomegranate, Box 6099, Rohnert Park, CA 94927

Great Authors

Nelson Algren (American, 1909–1981) observed the Great Depression and wrote about it in his first novel, *Somebody in Boots*. His observations of poverty and crime among the Poles of Chicago's West Side became his second book, *Never Come Morning*. *The Man with the Golden Arm*, a gritty portrayal of the world of petty crime and drug addiction, was a best-seller and won the 1949 National Book Award.

Pomegranate, Box 6099, Rohnert Park, CA 94927

Great Authors

Countee Cullen (American, 1903–1946). One of the
strongest voices associated with the Harlem Renais-
sance of the 1920s, Countee Cullen was widely
celebrated from the publication of his first book, *Color*.
After receiving a master's degree from Harvard, Cullen
became an editor and critic and later delved into the
writing of plays and novels. But it was his poetry that
singled him out as a voice to be listened to.

Pomegranate, Box 6099, Rohnert Park, CA 94927

Great Authors

Oscar Wilde (Irish, 1854–1900). The author of the classic comedy *The Importance of Being Earnest*, the charming fairy tales collected in *The Happy Prince,* and many aphorisms, essays and letters, Wilde is perhaps best remembered for the personal tragedy reflected in the poems "The Ballad of Reading Gaol" and "De Profundis." "There is only one thing in the world worse than being talked about," he wrote in *The Picture of Dorian Gray,* "and that is not being talked about."

Pomegranate, Box 6099, Rohnert Park, CA 94927

Great Authors

Lillian Hellman (American, 1905–1984). The intense drama of Hellman's plays (*The Little Foxes*, *Watch on the Rhine*) and the rich texture of her memoirs (*An Unfinished Woman, Pentimento*) stand as testaments to her independent views and her psychological insight. During the McCarthy witch hunts of the 1950s Hellman told the House Un-American Activities Committee that she would not "cut her conscience to fit this year's fashion," and she was not forced to testify.

Pomegranate, Box 6099, Rohnert Park, CA 94927

Great Authors

James Mallahan Cain (American, 1892–1977) is most
famous for *The Postman Always Rings Twice*, a taut, best-
selling tale of lust and murder that was made, and
remade, into riveting films. Two of his other best-
known works, *Double Indemnity* and *Mildred Pierce*, also
filmed, were prime examples of Cain's slam-bang style.
While he was considered by many critics to be a creator
of mere tabloid entertainments, Cain was imitated by
many writers of greater literary reputation, among them
Albert Camus in *The Stranger*.

Pomegranate, Box 6099, Rohnert Park, CA 94927

Great Authors
Anton Pavlovich Chekhov (Russian, 1860–1904), a
medical doctor and writer, was often forced to create in
the midst of chaos—the demands of patients; the
arguments of the family he supported; the rebellions of
his own body, wracked by tuberculosis. The vast sweep
of Russia under uneasy skies, snowstorms, love affairs,
the ticking of clocks and the wasting of lives, a little
hope and laughter: these are the elements found in
Chekhov's masterful stories.

Pomegranate, Box 6099, Rohnert Park, CA 94927

Great Authors

H. D. (Hilda Doolittle, American, 1886–1961). Hilda Doolittle's poetry was labeled by fiancé Ezra Pound, who scrawled "H. D. Imagiste" across the bottom of one of her first poems. Influenced by the mythologies of Greece and Egypt and by her own Moravian background, H. D. remained associated with the imagist movement, constructing poems of delicate complexity over the foundation of her experiences—including marriage to and divorce from writer Richard Aldington, psychoanalysis by Sigmund Freud and a long, tension-filled relationship with Winifred Ellerman.

Pomegranate, Box 6099, Rohnert Park, CA 94927

Photograph by Man Ray, c. 1923
Prints and Photographs Division

Great Authors

James Baldwin's (American, 1924–1987) powerful plays and novels include *Blues for Mr. Charlie*, *Go Tell It on the Mountain* and *Tell Me How Long the Train's Been Gone*. A Holy Roller preacher at fourteen, a writer from the age of twenty-one, an African American whose first novel was completed after he had settled in Paris, Baldwin described a world of struggle and prejudice in vibrant prose. His *The Fire Next Time* has been called one of the most powerful indictments of racial tyranny and confusion ever written.

Pomegranate, Box 6099, Rohnert Park, CA 94927

Great Authors

Henry James (American, 1843–1916). A "detached observer" of the manners of the upper-class society in which he moved, James produced twenty full-length novels, twelve novellas (including the classic *The Turn of the Screw*) and more than a hundred short stories, as well as plays, travel sketches, essays and reviews. He was an important force in the development of modern American and European literature.

Pomegranate, Box 6099, Rohnert Park, CA 94927

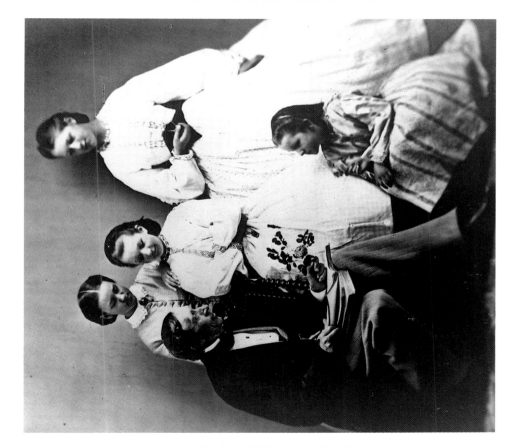

Great Authors

Hans Christian Andersen (Danish, 1805–1875). All of
the heroes of Andersen's 156 fairy tales have something
of the author in them: the Little Mermaid, rejected by
the world above her mysterious deep; the child who
knows the Emperor has no clothes; the Ugly Duckling;
the Little Fir Tree. Part autobiography, these stories are
also part of the rich tradition of Scandinavian
storytelling. Andersen also wrote six novels and a
wealth of excellent travel books, but he will always be
remembered for his consummate skill at relating tales of
the imagination.

Pomegranate, Box 6099, Rohnert Park, CA 94927

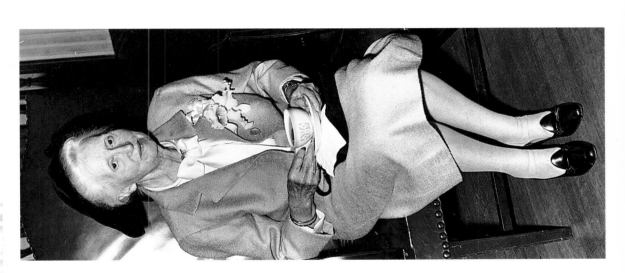

Great Authors
Marianne Craig Moore (American, 1887–1972). A
mosaicist in words, Moore created her own disciplined
verse from countless small observations: the baseball
player; imperial floor coverings of coach-wheel yellow;
the flamingo-colored, maple leaf–like feet of a swan
under the willows in Oxford. Moore entered the world
of poetry by contributing to the English magazine *The
Egoist*. Volumes of poetry followed and, following
them, awards and honors. "Poetry," she said, "watches
life with affection."

Pomegranate, Box 6099, Rohnert Park, CA 94927

Photograph taken at a reception at the Library of Congress,
1963

Great Authors

William Faulkner (American, 1897–1962). Complex in person as well as in his frustratingly intricate novels (*The Sound and the Fury; Light in August; Absalom, Absalom!*), Faulkner held to his faith in humankind while creating characters that one critic called "twisted shapes in the chaotic wreckage of a mad world." His eloquence on the role of the writer was countered by reticence concerning the process of writing. "If a story is in you," he said simply, "it has got to come out."

Pomegranate, Box 6099, Rohnert Park, CA 94927

Great Authors

W. (William) Somerset Maugham (British, 1874–1965) was a doctor who practiced medicine for only one year, as an intern in a slum neighborhood. The result of this experience was his first book, *Liza of Lambeth*. Though his first success was as a playwright, it is for his stories and novels, particularly *Of Human Bondage*, *The Moon and Sixpence* and *The Razor's Edge*, that he is best remembered. Haughty, compassionate, warm, acidic, witty, reticent, a vigorous traveler, prone to bad health, Maugham once said, "There are three rules for writing a novel. Unfortunately, no one knows what they are."

Pomegranate, Box 6099, Rohnert Park, CA 94927

Great Authors

Zora Neale Hurston (American, 1891–1960). Among the novels Hurston produced are *Mules and Men*, *Their Eyes Were Watching God* and *Seraph on the Suwannee*. *Dust Tracks on a Road*, a dramatic description of her family, her childhood and her struggle for an education, won the Anisfield award for better race relations. About her decision to complement her work as a folklorist with the creation of fiction, Hurston said: "I saw that what was being written by Negro authors was all on the same theme—the race problem. . . . I made up my mind to write about my people as they are, and not to use the traditional lay figures."

Pomegranate, Box 6099, Rohnert Park, CA 94927

Great Authors

Thomas Wolfe (American, 1900–1938) poured out his
memories and dreams in undisciplined manuscripts of
larger-than-epic proportions, which the dedication of
skilled editors—particularly the famed Maxwell
Perkins—carved into novels of acceptable length and
cohesion. *Look Homeward Angel*, *Of Time and the River*
and *You Can't Go Home Again* drew directly from his
own life and experiences. Regret, hunger, loneliness and
visions sang in the huge music of his prose.

Pomegranate, Box 6099, Rohnert Park, CA 94927

Great Authors

Willa Cather (American, 1876–1947) moved to Red
Cloud, Nebraska, from Virginia when she was eight
and thrived on the sparse semi-pioneer life of that land.
She studied the English classics and Latin with her
grandmothers at home, encountering her first strong
literary influence in the works of Virgil. The novels she
created as she grew into the literary life—including the
classics *O Pioneers!*, *My Antonia* and *Death Comes to the
Archbishop*—reflect this influence in their economy of
expression, their grace, their feeling for the past and
their undramatic sense of the sorrows that lie hidden in
every day.

Pomegranate, Box 6099, Rohnert Park, CA 94927

Great Authors

Mark Twain (Samuel Langhorne Clemens, American,
1835–1910), with John Lewis. Mark Twain's views on
the human race tended to be a trifle jaundiced—which
was not necessarily a negative trait, as it added
electricity to the humor in his speeches, stories and
novels (such as *The Adventures of Huckleberry Finn* and *A
Connecticut Yankee in King Arthur's Court*). Some
enduring relationships belied his dark view of
humankind, among them his friendship with tenant
farmer John Lewis, who rescued three of Mark Twain's
relatives from a runaway carriage.

Pomegranate, Box 6099, Rohnert Park, CA 94927

Great Authors

Knut Hamsun (Norwegian, 1859–1952). For his first thirty years, Hamsun was a wanderer, largely self-educated, taking odd jobs, living from hand to mouth. He started to write at nineteen, and in 1888 he published fragments of his first novel, *Hunger*. They caused a sensation and established him as a writer. A deeply reticent, conservative man, Hamsun was a lover of nature and, in his books, an explorer of human psychology. Other novels include *Pan* and *The Growth of the Soil*.

Pomegranate, Box 6099, Rohnert Park, CA 94927

Great Authors

W.E.B. (William Edward Burghardt) Du Bois (American, 1868–1963) was an impassioned scholar, an intellectual warrior on behalf of true citizenship for African Americans. Educated at Fisk University and Harvard, Du Bois wrote histories, sociological studies, informed sketches of Negro life and an autobiography. Editor, teacher and organizer as well as writer, he organized the First International Congress of Colored People and was a founder of the NAACP. Toward the end of his life, Du Bois grew discouraged with his struggles in the United States, and in 1961 he moved to Ghana, becoming a citizen there the year of his death.

Pomegranate, Box 6099, Rohnert Park, CA 94927

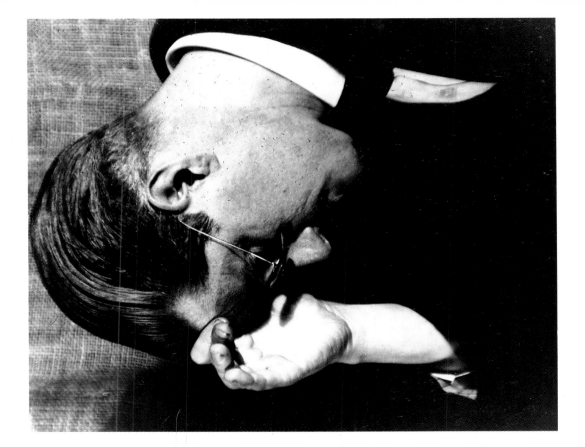

Great Authors

James Joyce (Irish, 1882–1941). A virtuoso in English (fluent in over a dozen other languages as well) whose major works are known for their obscurity and difficulty, a writer of epic manuscripts whose eye trouble made him nearly blind, a courtly family man who dressed with conservative elegance—and whose epic work *Ulysses* was for years vilified as "the foulest book that has ever found its way into print"—James Joyce embraced writing early and expended his life creating in words his own immense, many-faceted vision.

Pomegranate, Box 6099, Rohnert Park, CA 94927

Photograph by Man Ray, c. 1940
Prints and Photographs Division